KIDS
YOGA CLASS
IDEAS

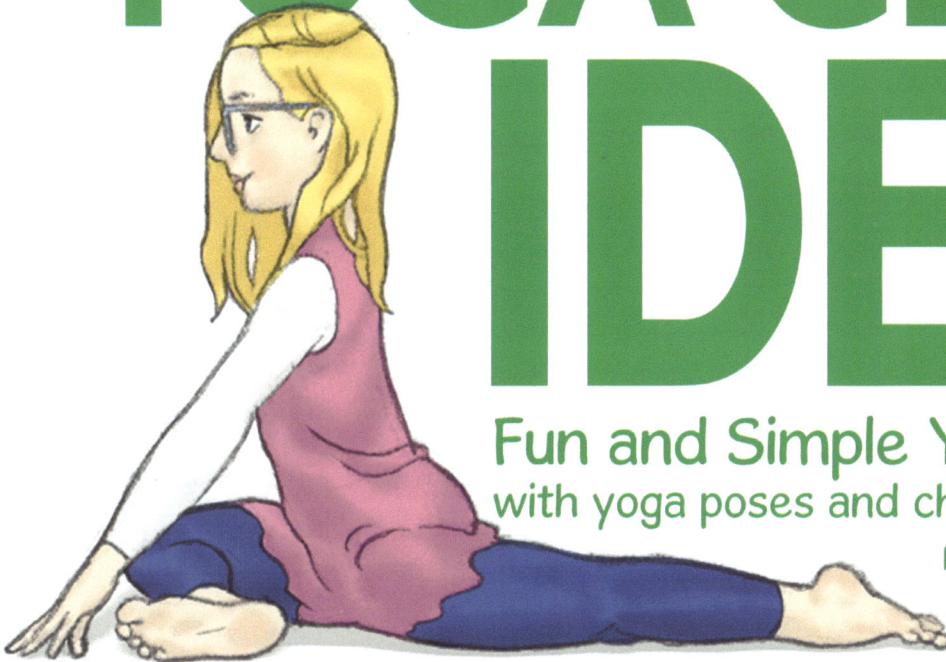

Fun and Simple Yoga Themes
with yoga poses and children's book
recommendations
for each month

Giselle Shardlow
www.KidsYogaStories.com

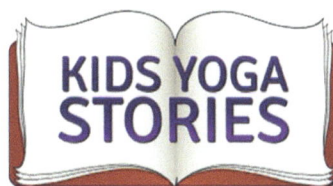

KIDS YOGA STORIES

www.kidsyogastories.com

ISBN: 978-1-943648-25-2

Kids Yoga Stories
Boston, MA
www.kidsyogastories.com
www.amazon.com/author/giselleshardlow

Email us at info@kidsyogastories.com.

What do you think? Let us know what you think of *Kids Yoga Class Ideas* at feedback@kidsyogastories.com.

WELCOME TO KIDS YOGA CLASS IDEAS

Are you looking for fun kids yoga ideas?

This book is for primary school teachers, kids yoga teachers, parents, caregivers, health practitioners, and recreation staff looking for fun, simple ways to add yoga to their curriculum, classes, or home life.

To spark your imagination, each monthly theme includes:

- Five yoga poses for kids

- Five recommended children's books

Each theme offers an opportunity to explore a topic through movement. These yoga themes are designed for children ages three to eight, but they could be adapted for younger or older children. Many of the topics are common in standard preschool and kindergarten classroom curriculums, as well as being special topics of interest for young children.

Each session could last between fifteen and forty-five minutes, depending on the needs and requirements of the children participating. The yoga poses are sequenced in a logical format to invite flow from one pose to the next. In preparation for your fun yoga experience, feel free to gather props and information on the lesson's topic. Use resources such as YouTube clips, newspaper articles, magazine pictures, old calendar pictures, Internet sites, guest speakers, brochures, and fiction and non-fiction books to expand the lesson as you see fit.

To make your yoga experience as successful as possible:

- Focus on having fun with movement, not on practicing perfectly aligned poses.

- Engage the children.

- Follow their passions and interests.

- Create authentic, meaningful experiences.

- Cater to their energy levels and different learning styles.

- Be creative and enjoy yourself—the kids will notice your enthusiasm.

- Encourage children to make up their own yoga stories using the five yoga poses.

- Brainstorm other yoga poses that fit each theme.

- Wear comfortable clothing and practice barefoot.

- Make safety a top priority—clear the space of obstacles and be safe with your bodies.

- Encourage the children to share their yoga experiences with their families and friends.

- Use the ideas in this book as a springboard and add other age-appropriate theme-related yoga poses, songs, breathing techniques, relaxation stories, or meditations.

Get children learning, moving, and having fun with these fun and simple kids yoga class ideas!

TABLE OF CONTENTS

BALLET YOGA

Pretend to be ballet dancers warming up for practice. Then learn the five basic first positions and other ballet moves like *pas de chat*, *arabesque*, *jeté*, *pirouette*, and *plie* with the book suggestions.

TREE POSE
Practice balancing on one foot.
Stand tall in Mountain Pose. Then shift to standing on one leg, bend your knee, place the sole of your foot on your opposite inner thigh, and balance. Repeat on the other side. Talk about how Tree Pose can help ballerinas practice balancing while keeping their heads up and backs straight.

DANCER'S POSE
Practice back bending.
Come back to Mountain Pose. Then stand on your right leg, reach your left leg out behind you, and place the outside of your left foot into your left hand. Bend your torso forward, keeping your right arm out in front for balance, and arch your left leg up behind you. Think about reaching far forward while gently bending your back and lifting your leg high behind you. Imagine flying across the stage like a ballerina. Return to Mountain Pose and repeat the steps on the other side.

BOAT POSE
Practice strengthening your core.
Come to sitting with a tall spine and your legs bent. Lean back slightly, take your arms straight out parallel in front of you, balance on your buttocks, and lift your straightened legs to forty-five-degree angle in front of you. Keep a tall spine and tighten your belly. Think of strengthening your core in preparation for more difficult ballet moves.

SEATED FORWARD BEND
Practice forward bending.
Come to sitting on your buttocks with your legs straight out in front of you. Bend your torso forward, keeping your spine straight, and gently reach toward your toes. Imagine being a ballerina who is practicing forward bends to increase your flexibility and stretch your spine. You could also practice pointing and flexing your toes.

EASY POSE
Practice sitting tall.
Cross your legs and rest your hands on your knees. Take your shoulders back, open your chest, and sit tall. Gently bring your knees to the ground and slowly open your hips. You could also practice stretching to each side to open up the sides of your body. Close your eyes if that's comfortable (or gaze down in front of you). Take a few deep breaths. Imagine being a ballet dancer leaping and twirling across the floor. Imagine what your costume would look like and what music would be playing for your special dance.

BALLET BOOKS

Tallulah's Tutu
by Marilyn Singer and Alexandra Boiger
Tallulah is a strong-willed girl who is determined to earn a tutu in her ballet class. She eventually learns that earning a tutu through consistent effort is worth the wait.
Ages 4+

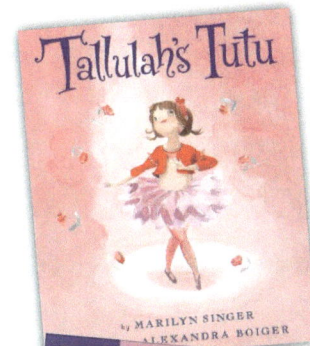

Little Ballet Star
by Adele Geras and Shelagh McNicholas
This darling ballet book is perfect for the young aspiring ballerina. In the story, Tilly's aunt is a professional ballerina who shows her how she gets ready for a ballet. For a birthday present, her aunt brings her up on stage as a surprise.
Ages 4+

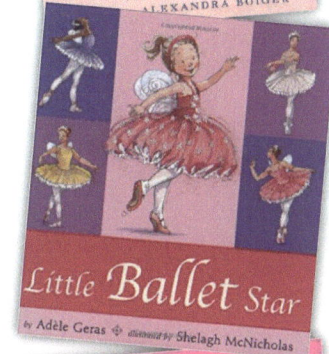

Josephine Wants to Dance
by Jackie French and Bruce Whatley
Josephine is an ambitious kangaroo who wants to join the local ballet. Through determination and perseverance, she earns the opportunity to play the main role.
Ages 3+

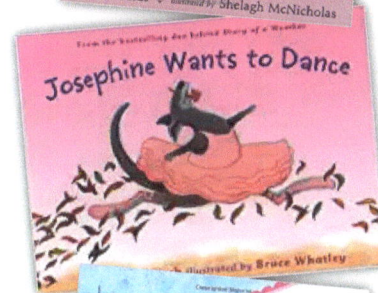

A Bunny in the Ballet
by Robert Beck
Désirée Rabbit loves to dance, but when she enters a ballet school in her hometown of Paris, the woman at the front desk declares, "There are no bunnies in the ballet!" The bunny proves her talents to the ballet class in this story of following your dreams.
Ages 4+

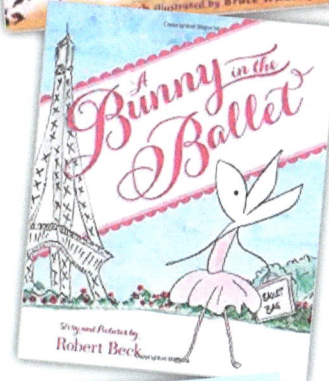

Amazing Grace
by Mary Hoffman and Caroline Binch
Grace loves acting out stories. When she hears that her class is planning a Peter Pan performance, she's determined to audition for the main part. This is an endearing story of a relationship between a girl, her mother, and her grandmother.
Ages 4+

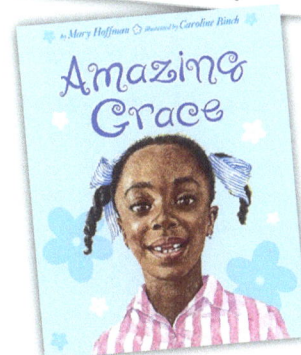

Valentine's Day is about who you love. Your children can first make a list of five people they would like to acknowledge in their "I Love You" Yoga sequence. For this "I Love You" Yoga sun salute sequence, students can use the example of honoring their mother, father, grandparents, and best friend.

EXTENDED MOUNTAIN POSE
Say "I love you, Momma!"
Stand tall in Mountain Pose, look up, and reach your arms up to the sky. Say, "I love you, Momma."

STANDING FORWARD BEND
Say "I love you, Dadda!"
From Mountain Pose, bend your upper body, keep a straight spine, and reach for your toes. Say, "I love you, Dadda."

DOWNWARD-FACING DOG POSE
Say "I love you, Grandma!"
Place both palms flat on the ground and step back with both feet so that you're in an upside-down V shape, with your buttocks high in the air. Straighten your legs, relax your head and neck, and look down between your legs. Say, "I love you, Grandma."

TABLE TOP POSE
Say "I love you, Grandpa!"
Shift forward and bring your knees gently to the ground in an all-fours position with your fingers spread out and palms flat on the ground. Ensure that your back and neck are in a straight but neutral position. Your shoulders should be over your wrists, and your hips should be over your knees. The tops of your feet are flat on the ground. Say, "I love you, Grandpa."

CHILD'S POSE
Say "I love you, friends!"
Come back to sit on your heels, slowly bring your forehead down to rest in front of your knees, and rest your arms down alongside your body. Say, "I love you, [name of your best friend]." Take a few deep breaths, thinking about all the special people in your life.

Because Your Grandparents Love You

by Andrew Clements and R.W. Alley

This darling book demonstrates the unconditional love of grandparents. Also, check out the Mommy and Daddy versions in the same series. Lyrical text and charming illustrations.

Ages 4+

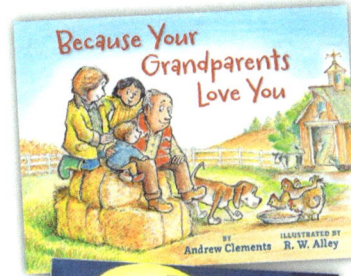

Mama, Do You Love Me?

by Barbara M. Joose and Barbara Lavallee

This story shows how a mother's love is deep and unconditional, even as the child pushes for her own independence. The illustrations of Alaska are beautiful.

Ages 2+

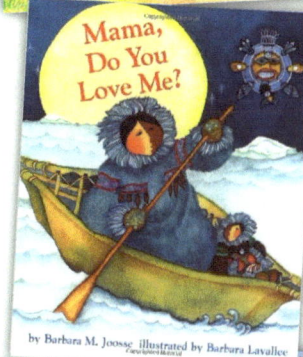

Love You Forever

by Robert Munsch and Sheila McGraw

This heartfelt classic belongs on every child's bookshelf. Readers recite the song that the mother sings to her baby, "I'll love you forever, I'll like you for always, As long as I'm living, My baby you'll be."

Ages 4+

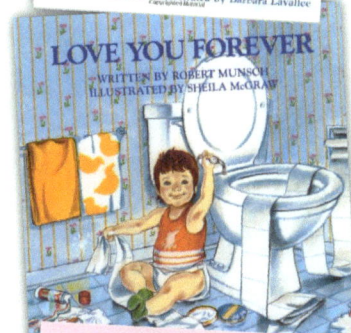

Foxy in Love

by Emma Dodd

This fun-loving story follows Emily as her friend, Foxy, helps her put together a Valentine's Day card filled with all the things that she loves most.

Ages 4+

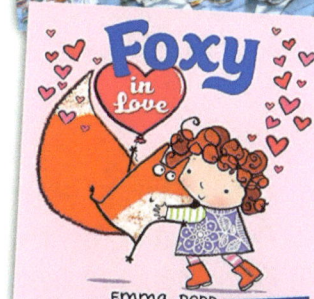

The I LOVE YOU Book

by Todd Parr

The famous author-illustrator celebrates the ways in which parents and children love each other. Young readers will love the simple, engaging text and bright, colorful illustrations.

Ages 2+

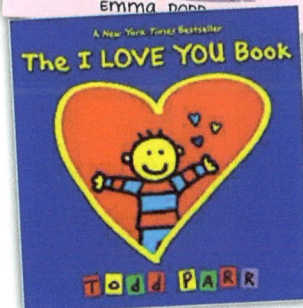

WEATHER YOGA

We found more than forty children's books about weather at our local library, so there's plenty of inspiration out there for the kids to invent their own weather yoga poses to add to this sequence. Brainstorm a list of weather words—like clouds, rain, or sunshine—to act out through yoga poses for kids.

EXTENDED MOUNTAIN POSE
Pretend to be the sun.

Stand tall in Mountain Pose, inhale, look up, take your arms straight up to the sky, and say hello to the sun. You can then exhale and bring your arms back down alongside your body. Repeat the inhale and exhale pattern, raising and lowering your arms, for a few breaths and imagine sending out rays of sunshine.

TREE POSE
Pretend to be the wind.

Stand on one leg. Bend the knee of the leg you are not standing on, place the sole of your foot on the opposite inner thigh or calf (but not your knee), and balance. Sway like a tree in the wind. Switch sides and repeat the steps.

CHAIR POSE
Pretend to be a lightning bolt.

Stand tall with your feet hip-width apart, bend your knees, and keep a straight spine. Hold your hands up in front of you with straight arms, pretending to be a lightning bolt.

STANDING FORWARD BEND
Pretend to be the rain.

From Mountain Pose, bend your upper body, keep a straight spine, and reach for your toes. Pretend your arms are falling raindrops.

CHILD'S POSE
Pretend to be a snowflake.

Sit back on your heels, slowly bring your forehead down to rest on the floor in front of your knees, rest your arms down alongside your body, and take a few deep breaths. Pretend to be a **snowflake** falling from the sky. Take a few deep breaths.

Cloudy with a Chance of Meatballs

by Judi Barrett and Ron Barrett

This book was my daughter's favorite weather book, and I used to read it in my primary classrooms. The weather in the town of Chewandswallow brings weather three times a day (breakfast, lunch, and dinner) to serve up food for its residents. Kids find it hilarious!

Ages 4+

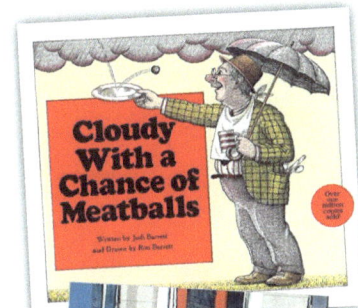

SNOW

by Sam Usher

The story builds anticipation as a young boy is waiting patiently for his grandfather to get ready so they can be the first to play in the freshly fallen snow. The book is a great introduction to a discussion about patience.

Ages 3+

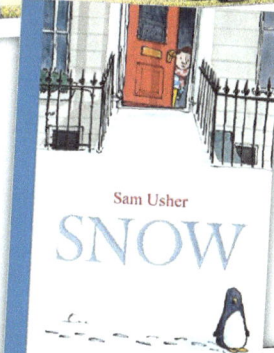

The Umbrella

by Jan Brett

This story follows a boy who puts down his umbrella while in search of rainforest animals on a rainy day in the cloud forest. Meanwhile, a group of animals all huddle together in the abandoned umbrella.

Ages 4+

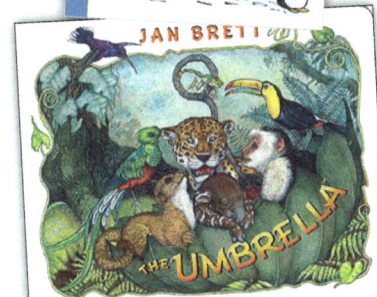

The Wind Blew

by Pat Hutchins

This charming book shows how a group of townspeople lose their things in the blustery wind. My daughter screeched with laughter throughout the whole book.

Ages 3+

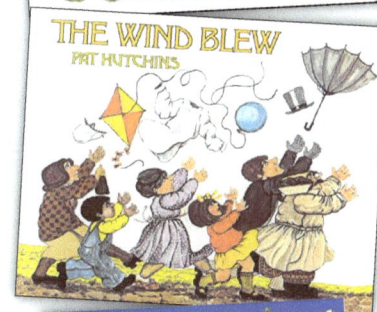

You Are My Sunshine

by Steve Metzger and Jill Dubin

I've been singing this song to my daughter since she was born. She still asks for this book, and it's a great way to cuddle up to read together.

Ages 1+

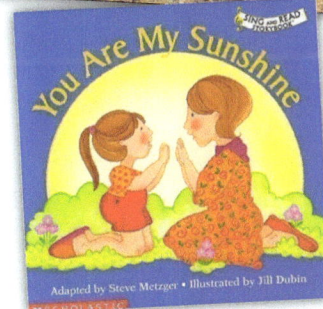

FEELINGS YOGA

Talk about managing your emotions through movement. Try imitating these animals through yoga poses for kids to help lighten the topic of emotions. Make up your own feelings yoga poses for other emotions like sad, silly, or angry.

EXTENDED MOUNTAIN POSE
A grateful giraffe returns to the wild.

Stand tall in Mountain Pose, look up, take your arms straight up to the sky, and touch your palms together. Pretend your arms a giraffe's long neck.

TREE POSE
A finicky flamingo picks at a snack.

Stand on your right leg. Bend the knee your left leg, place the sole of your left foot on your right inner thigh or calf (not your knee), and balance. Pretend to be a flamingo picking at its snack. Switch sides and repeat the steps.

EAGLE POSE
A caring koala cuddles her baby.

Stand tall in Mountain Pose. Wrap your left leg around your right. Bring your bent arms out in front of you, wrap your right arm around your left arm, and bend your knees slightly. Pretend to be a momma koala cuddling her baby. Switch sides and repeat the steps.

WIDE-LEGGED FORWARD BEND
An excited elephant runs to the waterhole.

Stand tall with legs hip-width apart, feet facing forward, and straighten your arms alongside your body. Step your feet out wide, bend your upper body, clasp your hands together, and pretend your arms are an elephant's trunk. Take your clasped hands up overhead (inhale), making the excited sound of an elephant, then bring your clasped hands down (exhale), pretending to drink from the waterhole.

SQUAT POSE
A frustrated frog can't catch a fly.

Come down to a squat with your knees apart and your arms between your knees. Touch your hands to the ground. Jump up like a frog trying to catch a fly and then come back to a squat position.

Have You Filled a Bucket Today?

by Carol McCloud and David Messing

This famous book is used by families and schools to talk to children about specific behaviors that "fill" or "dip" into each other's buckets.

Ages 4+

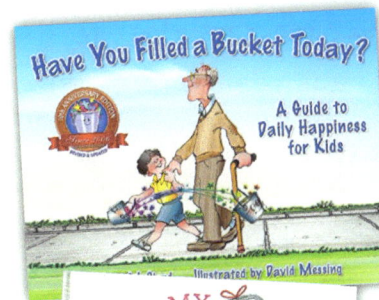

In My Heart: A Book of Feelings

by Jo Witek and Christine Roussey

This simple and sweet book introduces children to various feelings.

Ages 2+

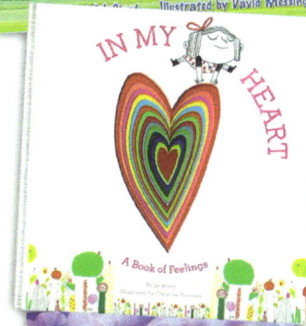

Visiting Feelings

by Lauren Rubenstein and Shelly Hehenberger

This beautifully illustrated book has an endearing message that feelings come and go.

Ages 5+

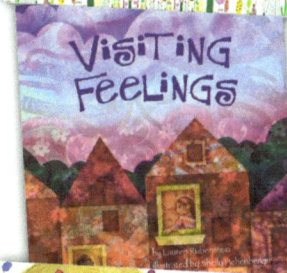

Today I Feel Silly
& Other Moods That Make My Day

by Jamie Lee Curtis and Laura Cornell

The author and illustrator have done a great job of appealing visually to young children, who will also love the rhyming text.

Ages 4+

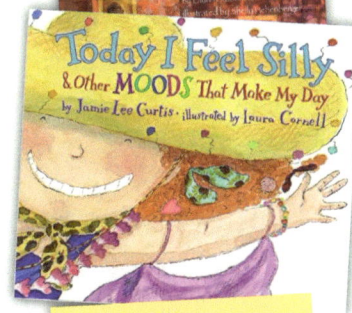

Anh's Anger

by Gail Silver and Christiane Kromer

This story is about a boy who imagines talking to his anger to calm himself.

Ages 4+

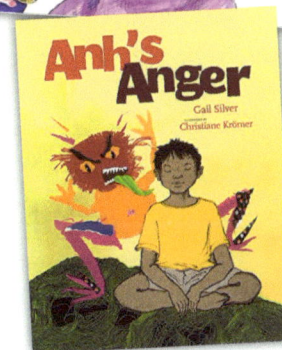

NOCTURNAL ANIMALS YOGA

The night animals featured in these poses are common in the northeastern part of the United States, but feel free to adapt to the night animals near you. After looking at books, you could make a list of animals that are active at night.

STANDING FORWARD BEND
Pretend to be a bat.
Stand tall with legs hip-width apart, feet facing forward, and straighten your arms alongside your body. Bend your upper body, reach for your toes, and pretend to hang upside-down like a bat.

SQUAT POSE
Pretend to be a toad.
Come down to a squat with your knees apart and your arms between your knees. Touch your hands to the ground. Jump up like a toad and then come back to a squat position. Repeat the toad hop a few times.

EXTENDED CAT POSE
Pretend to be a fox.
Come to all fours, extend one leg out behind you, and look forward. Take the opposite arm out in front of you to counter-balance. Pretend to be a fox dashing through the forest. Repeat on the other side.

DOWNWARD-FACING DOG POSE
Pretend to be a coyote.
Step back to your hands and feet, with your buttocks up in the air, creating a V shape. Stretch like a coyote.

HERO POSE
Pretend to be an owl.
Come to rest upright on your heels, with your palms resting on your knees. Twist your upper body like an owl turning its head. Turn your upper body one way and then the other.

Moon Child
by Nadia Krilanovich and Elizabeth Sayles
The simple and sweet text of this book might be good for a toddler or preschool yoga class to act out the various "moon child" animals.
Ages 3+

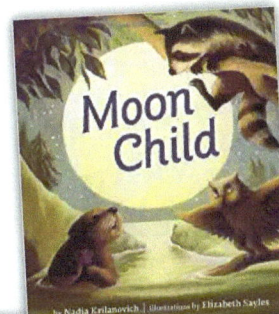

Whoo Goes There?
by Jennifer Ericsson and Bert Kitchen
An owl hears sounds from its perch in a tree and asks, "Whoo goes there?" Always hoping the sound will be a mouse for its dinner, the owl patiently watches other nocturnal animals scurrying around, making noises. Eventually, he sees a mouse, but it gets away.
Ages 2+

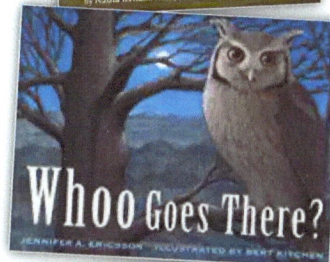

While the World is Sleeping
by Pamela Duncan Edwards and Daniel Kirk
This bedtime book follows a little boy who rides on the wings of an owl and takes a journey through the night to see what nocturnal animals do while the humans are sleeping.
Ages 4+

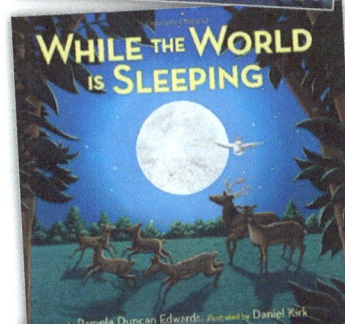

Where Are the Night Animals?
by Mary Ann Fraser
This non-fiction book explains how nocturnal animals are specially adapted to live in the dark.
Ages 4+

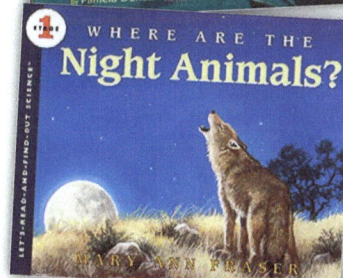

Night Animals
by Gianna Marino
A silly book featuring night animals who say they are scared of night animals and don't realize that they themselves are night animals. This book helps bring humor to the fear of the sounds outside at night.
Ages 3+

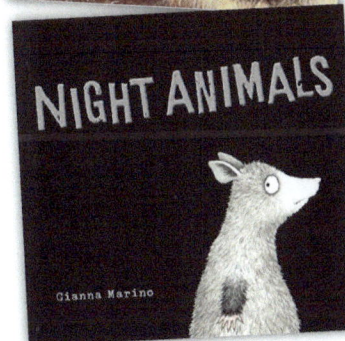

SHAPES YOGA

After reading the shapes books for kids, you can make a list of shape words that you'd like your child to learn. Let your inspiration take you beyond the usual lessons of circles and squares to curvy and straight lines, as well.

DOWNWARD-FACING DOG POSE
Pretend to be a triangle.
From Standing Forward Bend, step back to your hands and feet in an upside-down V shape, with your buttocks up in the air, and pretend to create a triangle shape. (You could also practice Triangle Pose to see a triangle created with your legs.) Say, "I'm a triangle!"

PLANK POSE
Pretend to be a rectangle.
From Downward-Facing Dog Pose, come forward to balance on your palms and on your bent toes, in a plank position. Keep your arms straight and your back long and flat. Imagine that you are creating a rectangle shape with your body. Say, "I'm a rectangle!"

TABLE TOP POSE
Pretend to be a square.
Drop your knees gently on the floor and come to an all-fours position with your fingers spread out and palms flat on the ground. Ensure that your back and neck are in a straight but neutral position. Your shoulders should be over your wrists, and your hips should be over your knees while the tops of your feet are flat on the ground. Pretend to create a square shape with your body. Say, "I'm a square!"

CHILD'S POSE
Pretend to be a circle.
Shift back to sitting on your heels. Slowly bring your forehead down to rest on the floor in front of your knees, rest your arms down alongside your body, and take a few deep breaths. Pretend to be a circle shape with your body. Say, "I'm a circle!"

RESTING POSE
Pretend to be a star.
Lie on your back with your arms and legs stretched way out, like a star. Say, "I'm a star!" Breathe deeply and rest.

The Shape Song Swingalong

by Steve Songs and David Sim

My daughter and I are big fans of SteveSongs, and he's great in live concert, by the way. So it's no surprise that this shapes book is our favorite. A singalong CD comes with the book, making this a winner in teaching children about shapes!

Ages 3+

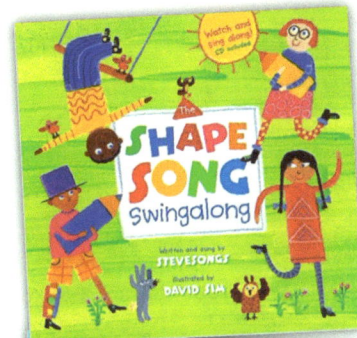

Ship Shapes

by Stella Blackstone and Siobhan Bell

Another great book by Barefoot Books, this one takes the reader on an artistic journey to the sea, looking for shapes on ships. This would be a fun book to read when you integrate your shapes and ocean units.

Ages 4+

Circle, Square, Moose

by Kelly Bingham and Paul O. Zelinsky

This is an absolutely silly book about shapes, where a zebra and moose keep interrupting the story. My daughter requests this book regularly and howls with laughter at each page.

Ages 4+

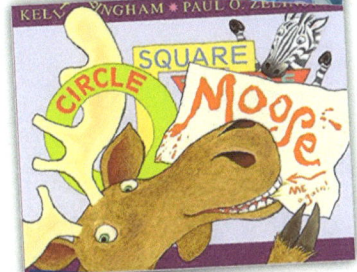

Round is Mooncake: A Book of Shapes

by Roseanne Thong and Grace Lin

This sweet book follows a girl who finds shapes in her urban neighborhood in China. Readers learn about shapes while experiencing an Asian country. For another setting, check out *Round is a Tortilla: A Book of Shapes* set in Latin America.

Ages 4+

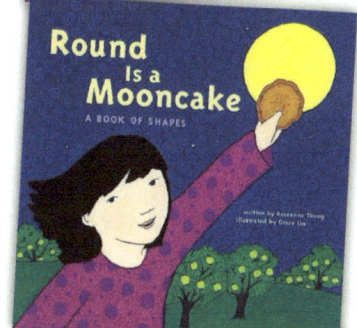

Bear in a Square

by Stella Blackstone and Debbie Harter

This cute little board book by Barefoot Books would be perfect to introduce shapes to infants and toddlers.

Ages 1+

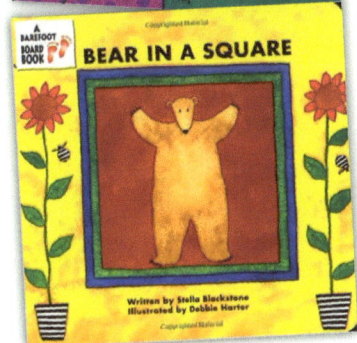

MERMAID YOGA

Take children on a journey to the magical and mysterious world of mermaids through these yoga poses for kids. As you go through the poses, talk about what they might see and hear in their pretend mermaid kingdom under the water. All of these poses all have the legs together, like a mermaid's tail.

HERO POSE
Pretend to be a mermaid sitting on a rock.
Come down to sit on your heels with your knees and toes touching. Place your hands in your knees, open your chest, and pretend to be a mermaid sitting on rock.

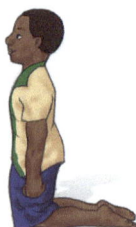

KNEELING POSE
Pretend to be a mermaid treading in the water.
Come up to stand on your knees, open your chest, and use your arms to pretend to tread gently in the ocean waters.

LOCUST POSE
Pretend to be a mermaid swimming through the water.
Take your hands down in front of you and lie on your tummy. Take your arms down alongside your body and stretch your legs straight behind you. Rest your forehand on the ground, making sure your neck and spine are elongated. For Locust Pose, lift your chest and shoulders, lift your hands back alongside you, look up, and pretend to be a mermaid gliding through the water.

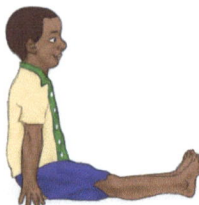

STAFF POSE
Pretend to be a mermaid relaxing on a sandy beach.
Come to a sitting position. Sit with a tall spine, with your legs straight out in front of you. Pretend to be a mermaid relaxing on a sandy beach, looking out over the ocean.

RESTING POSE
Pretend to a mermaid taking a rest on the ocean floor.
Shift back to lying on your back with your arms and legs stretched out. Breathe and rest. Imagine what kind of things and creatures you might see in the underwater mermaid world.

MERMAID BOOKS

The Singing Mermaid
by Julia Donaldson and Lydia Monks
This clever rhyming book follows a mermaid who is convinced to join a circus, but then her friends help her get back to the sea, where she belongs. The mean circus owner creates a teachable moment to talk about people who aren't friendly.
Ages 3+

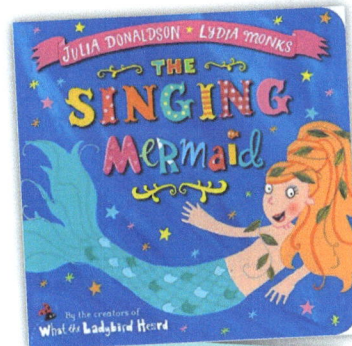

Fancy Nancy and the Mermaid Ballet
by Jane O'Connor and Robin Preiss Glasser
Fancy Nancy is disappointed about not getting the lead mermaid role in the dance show. She has to overcome her jealousy and find a way to embrace her role. This is a good book to read before a talk about competition and accepting what life gives you.
Ages 4+

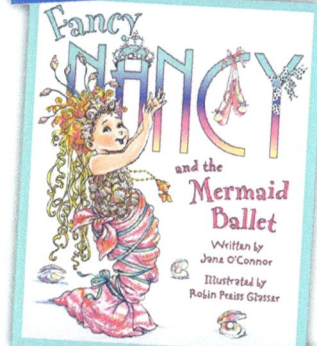

The Tiniest Mermaid
by Laura Garnham
This darling book follows a girl who rescues a hurt little mermaid and brings her home to look after her. The mermaid shows the girl her magical world of mermaids. This is a sweet story of friendship and enchanting worlds.
Ages 4+

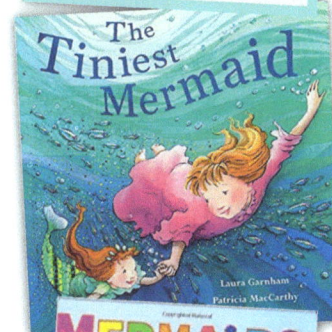

Mermaids on Parade
by Melanie Hope Greenberg
This fun, light-hearted book illustrates the yearly Mermaid Parade in New York City. This story is a great way to learn about that nation's largest art parade, which promotes self-expression, artistic expression, and community involvement. Who knew!
Ages 3+

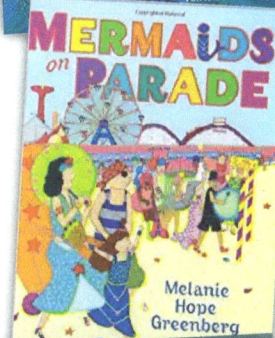

The Mermaid and the Shoe
by K.G. Campbell
Little Minnow is the only one of her fifty sisters who doesn't seem to have a special talent, except asking lots of questions. It's a sweet story of finding one's purpose.
Ages 3+

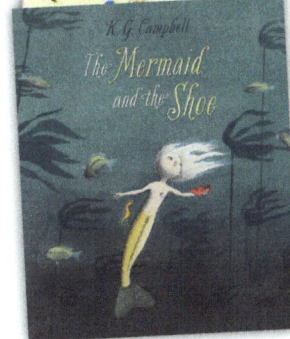

CAMPING YOGA

Brainstorm a list of things you might see and do on a camping trip, then act out your trip. You'll find all five of these poses in the Kids Yoga Stories *Yoga Poses for Kids Cards pack (Deck Two)* within the camping category of yoga cards.

TABLE TOP POSE
Pretend to be a tent.
Come to an all-fours position with your fingers spread out and palms flat on the ground. Ensure that your back and neck are in a straight but neutral position. Your shoulders should be over your wrists, and your hips should be over your knees while the tops of your feet are flat on the ground. Pretend to be a tent in a campground.

LEGS UP THE WALL
Pretend to be a lantern.
Lie flat on your back then slowly raise your legs straight up toward the sky, making an L shape with your body. Keeping your legs together, flex your feet. Spread your arms out to either side and keep your neck in a neutral position. You could also rest your legs up a wall instead. Pretend to be a lantern lighting up the campsite.

LOTUS POSE
Pretend to be a moonflower.
Sit with a tall spine, cross your legs, and rest the palms of your hands on your knees. Relax and breathe. Pretend to be a moonflower blooming at night.

CRESCENT MOON POSE
Pretend to be the moon.
Stand tall with legs hip-width apart, feet facing forward, and straighten your arms alongside your body. Reach your arms high over your head, bringing your palms together. Tilt your upper body to one side, pretending to be the crescent moon. Come back to center. Tilt your body to the other side.

WIDE-LEGGED FORWARD BEND
Pretend to be a woodchopper.
Stand tall with legs hip-width apart, feet facing forward, and straighten your arms alongside your body. Step your feet out wide, bend your upper body, clasp your hands together, and pretend you are chopping firewood like a woodchopper.

CAMPING BOOKS

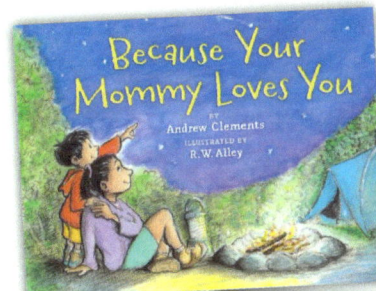

Because Your Mommy Loves You
by Andrew Clements and R.W. Alley
A mom encourages her son to be independent on their camping trip.
Ages 4+

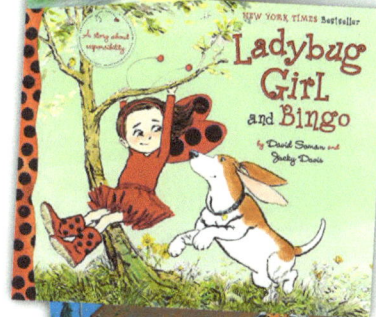

Ladybug Girl and Bingo
by David Soman and Jacky Davis
A young girl goes on a forest adventure with her dog on a family camping trip.
Ages 3+

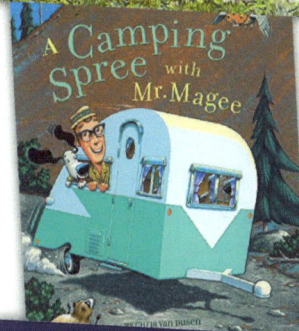

A Camping Spree by Mr. Magee
by Chris Van Dusen
A hilariously funny and engaging story of a man and his dog stuck in their camper van, which suddenly plunges down the mountain.
Ages 4+

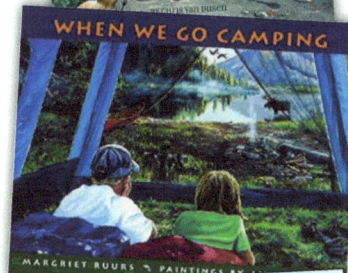

When We Go Camping
by Margriet Ruurs and Andrew Kiss
A family is busy exploring on their camping trip—the realistic illustrations are magnificent.
Ages 6+

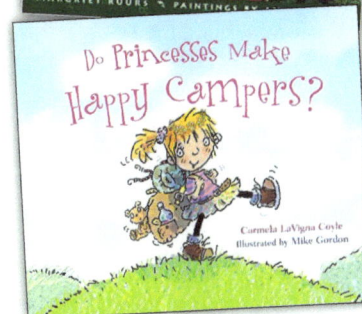

Do Princesses Make Happy Campers?
by Carmela LaVigna Coyle and Mike Gordon
A rhyming princess book that shows how to look on the bright side to become a happy camper.
Ages 3+

TRANSPORTATION YOGA

Talk with your children about the various modes of transportation, as well as where and how they might use them. Come up with yoga poses to match the modes of transportation. Try these poses found in the Kids Yoga Stories *Yoga Poses for Kids Cards pack (Deck One)* within the travel category of yoga cards.

BOAT POSE
Pretend to be a boat.

Balance on your buttocks with your arms and legs straight out in front of you, in a V shape. Keep a straight spine and an open chest. Then pretend to rock in the water like a boat.

PLANK POSE
Pretend to be a surfboard.

From Downward-Facing Dog Pose, come forward to balance on your palms and on your bent toes in a plank position. Keep your arms straight and your back long and flat. Pretend to be a surfboard skating across the water.

TRIANGLE POSE
Pretend to be a sailboat.

From a standing position, step one foot back, pointing your toe slightly outward. Take your arms up parallel to the ground, bend at your waist, and tilt your upper body to the side. Reach your front hand to gently rest on your shin and reach your other arm straight up. Pretend to be a sailboat gliding through the water. Switch sides and repeat the steps.

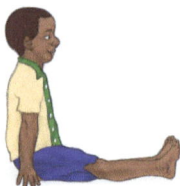

STAFF POSE
Pretend to be a train.

Sit with a tall spine and your legs straight out in front of you. Move your hands like the wheels of a train going down the track.

LUNGE POSE
Pretend to be a motorbike.

From Downward-Facing Dog Pose, step your right foot forward to rest just inside your right hand. Keep a flat back and open your chest. Pretend to be a motorbike cruising down the road. Switch sides and repeat the steps.

TRANSPORTATION BOOKS

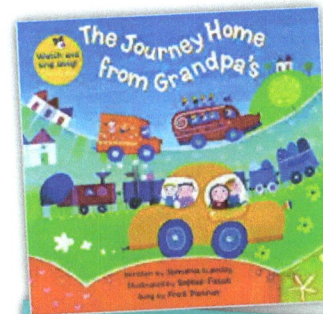

The Journey Home from Grandpa's
by Jemima Lumley and Sophie Fatus
Readers learn and sing about various modes of transportation on their way home from Grandpa's house.
Ages 4+

Lost and Found
by Oliver Jeffers
A darling story of a boy who makes, then loses, a friend penguin. Great to discuss the importance of love and friendships.
Ages 3+

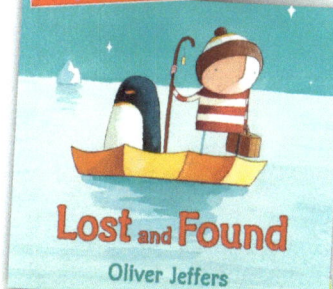

Duck in the Truck
by Jez Alborough
Read how Duck and friends try to get the truck out of the muck, all through hilarious rhyming text.
Ages 3+

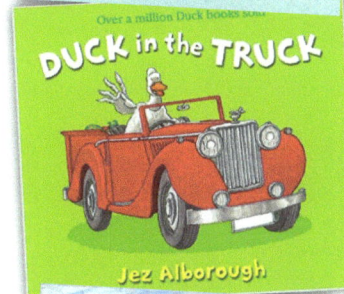

The Caboose that Got Loose
by Bill Peet
Katy Caboose doesn't like being at the back of the train and longs for peace and quiet. Then one day, her rusty bolts set her free from the train, and she ends up unexpectedly getting stuck in a tree. The story is a fun read with older children.
Ages 4+

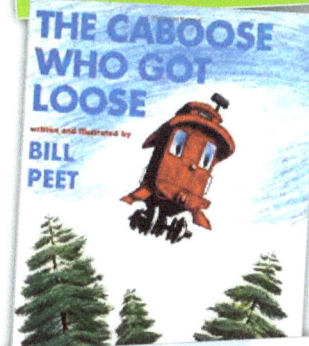

Wheels on the Bus
by Raffi and Sylvie Wickstrom
Sweet illustrations coupled with Raffi's jovial singing makes this book and CD a great combination.
Ages 1+

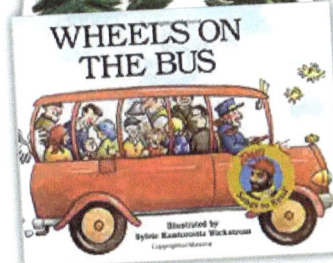

CIRCUS YOGA

Bring the circus to life at home, in your studio, or in your classroom with these circus-inspired yoga poses for children. Then your yoginis can invent new yoga poses mimicking circus performers that they have seen themselves, read about in circus books, or made up in their imaginations.

TREE POSE
Pretend to be balancing on a tight rope.
Stand on one leg. Bend your right knee, place the sole of your left foot on your right inner thigh or calf (not the knee), and balance. Pretend to be balancing on a tight rope. Switch sides and repeat the steps.

HORSE STANCE
Pretend to be lifting heavy weights.
Stand with your legs apart, feet facing slightly outward. Bend your knees and stand firm as if you're lifting a heavy weight above your head. Or you could pretend that you have another circus performer standing on your shoulders.

LUNGE
Pretend to be doing the splits.
From Horse Stance, come to a standing position. Then, on an exhale, do a swan dive to a Standing Forward Bend. Place your palms flat on the ground. Inhale, and on an exhale, step your right foot back into a lunge, bending deeply into your front left knee while ensuring that your knee is aligned above your ankle. Keep a flat back and open your chest. Pretend to be warming up to do the splits. You could certainly do the splits if that's available to you. Switch sides and repeat the steps.

DOWNWARD-FACING DOG POSE
Pretend to be getting ready to do a handstand.
Step back to your hands and feet in an upside-down V shape, with your buttocks up in the air. Check that your palms are flat on the ground and that your fingers are spread out evenly. Stay here or take baby steps forward to bring your torso right over your arms in preparation for a handstand. Again, you could do a full handstand if you're able.

LOCUST POSE
Pretend to be a trapeze performer reaching for the next swing.
Lie on your tummy, lift your chest and shoulders, and look up. Pretend you are a trapeze performer flying from one swing to another. You could also extend up into a full Bow Pose.

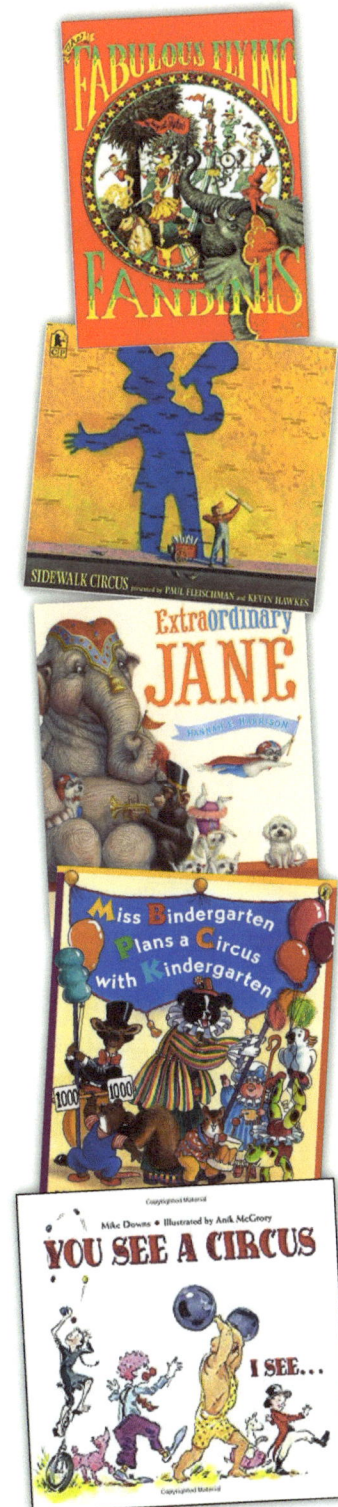

Fabulous Flying Fandinis

by Ingrid Slyder

Bobby's new neighbors welcome him into their house, which has been converted into a circus, complete with trapeze swings and exotic animals.

Ages 3+

Sidewalk Circus

by Paul Fleischman and Kevin Hawkes

This wordless book portrays how the everyday activities of people on the street are similar to the stunts of a circus performance.

Ages 5+

Extraordinary Jane

by Hannah E. Harrison

This story for young children follows a little dog living with the circus animals, who finds that her own ordinary-ness is uniquely extraordinary.

Ages 3+

Miss Bindergarten Plans a Circus with Kindergarten

by Joseph Slate and Ashley Wolff

This charming book is about an animal classroom that is planning a circus performance. Young children will enjoy the colorful illustrations and engaging rhyming text.

Ages 3+

You See A Circus, I See...

by Mike Downs and Anik McGory

This story is from the perspective of a little boy living a circus life. It's a great book to inspire discussion about how the perspective of a performer is different from a spectator's.

Ages 4+

FAIRY YOGA

Go on a magical journey through the land of fairies and follow this yoga sequence below or make up your own fairy story and matching fairy yoga sequence. Fairies might live in all kinds of places—even a fairy school or a secret garden.

DANCER'S POSE
Pretend to be dancing at the fairy ball.
Stand tall in Mountain Pose, stand on your right leg, reach your left leg out behind you, place the outside of your left foot into your left hand, bend your torso forward with your right arm out in front for balance, and arch your leg up behind you. Repeat on the other side. Pretend to be a dancing fairy.

WARRIOR 3 POSE
Pretend to be flying through the fairy forest.
Stand on your right leg. Extend your left leg behind you. Bend your torso forward and take your arms out to the sides to pretend you are flying through the fairy forest. Repeat on the other side.

LOCUST POSE
Pretend to swim near the fairy waterfall.
Lie on your tummy. Lift your chest and shoulders, look up, and rotate your bent arms in circles as if you are swimming through the waterfall pools.

COBBLER'S POSE
Pretend to flutter around the fairy garden.
Shift back to sit on your buttocks with a tall spine, bend your legs, place the soles of your feet together, and gently flap your legs like the wings of a butterfly. Pretend to flutter around the fairy flowers.

RESTING POSE
Pretend to sleep peacefully in the fairy palace.
Lie on your back with your arms and legs outstretched. Breathe and rest. Imagine you are resting in your cozy fairy bed in your fairy palace.

FAIRY BOOKS

The Dollhouse Fairy

by Jane Ray

Rosy and her dad love building furniture for her dollhouse. One day, Rosy finds a mischievous fairy living in her dollhouse. This is a sweet story of imagination and magical worlds.

Ages 3+

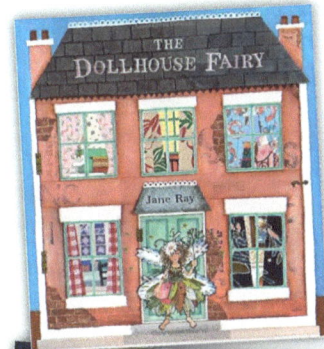

Fairy Houses

by Tracy Kane

Follow Kristen as she builds a fairy house in the woods. Read how other animals get involved in her adventure. Fairy house instructions are included at the back of the book.

Ages 5+

1001 Things to Spot in Fairyland

by Gillian Doherty, Anna Milbourne, and Teri Gower

Children can explore several magical fairy worlds—an enchanted waterfall, a fairy school, a secret garden, and a fairy palace—in this beautifully illustrated book.

Ages 5+

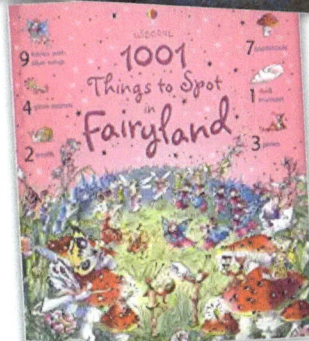

Where Do Fairies Go When It Snows?

by Liza Gardner Walsh and Hazel Mitchell

This is a darling rhyming book showing where fairies live all year round. Readers will enjoy the whimsical illustrations.

Ages 3+

Stella, Fairy of the Forest

by Marie-Louise Gay

Stella and Sam engage in a charming dialogue about fairies during their day in the woods. Stella uses her overactive imagination to answer her brother with creative and innocent answers. Check out other Stella book in this series.

Ages 2+

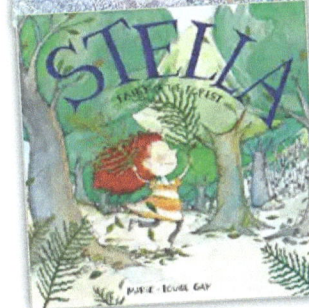

HOLIDAY YOGA

Imagine you are sitting in a cozy living room in front of a log fire, looking outside at the falling snow. Use these yoga poses to imagine the lights of the holiday season to bring you calm and peace. Follow this light-inspired yoga sequence or make up your own holiday yoga sequence.

STAR POSE (Variation of Mountain Pose)
Pretend to be a sparkling snowflake falling from the sky.
Stand tall with your legs hip-width apart and feet facing forward. Straighten your arms out alongside your body. Pretend to be a snowflake drifting down from the sky. Close your eyes (or gaze down in front of you) and take a few deep, calming breaths.

TREE POSE
Pretend to be a holiday tree with flashing lights.
Stand on your right leg, bend your knee, place the sole of your left foot on your right inner thigh, and balance. Pretend to be a Christmas tree with flashing lights and delightful decorations. Switch sides and repeat the pose on the other leg.

DANCER'S POSE
Pretend to be the moon lighting up the sky.
Stand tall in Mountain Pose. Then stand on your right leg, reach your left leg out behind you, place the outside of your left foot into your left hand, bend your torso forward with your right arm out in front for balance, and arch your leg up behind you. Imagine creating a moon shape with your outstretched leg. Pretend to be the moon shining over a forest of pine trees or a house filled with sleeping children.

CHAIR POSE
Pretend to be a candle flickering on the mantelpiece.
Stand tall in Extended Mountain Pose with your feet hip-width apart and your arms extended above you. Then, bend your knees and sink back as if you are sitting in a chair. Imagine that you are a white candle flickering light over your family. Hold the pose for a few rounds of deep breaths. You should start to feel heat in your body.

EASY POSE
Pretend to be a log fire with dancing flames.
Sit comfortably cross-legged and rest your hands on your knees. Close your eyes (or gaze down in front of you) and imagine that your crossed legs are the logs on the fire. With every extended inhale, imagine filling your body with fresh oxygen (fire). Simply focus on the sound of your breath and begin to quiet your mind.

CHRISTMAS BOOKS

Santa Duck

by David Milgrim

The best Christmas book for young children, for sure! It has a funny storyline and brilliant illustrations.

Ages 1 +

Bear Stays Up for Christmas

by Karma Wilson and Jane Chapman

Join Bear and his friends as they prepare for Christmas. This is a fabulous book for fans of the charming, rhyming Bear series by Karma Wilson.

Ages 2 +

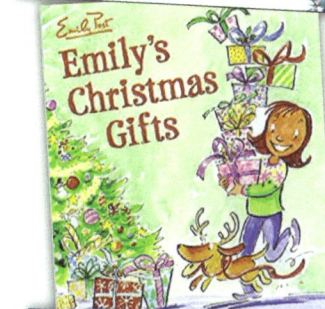

Emily's Christmas Gifts

by Cindy Post Senning, Peggy Post, and Steve Bjorkman

A lovely story of a little girl who gives the gift of kindness and consideration.

Ages 4 +

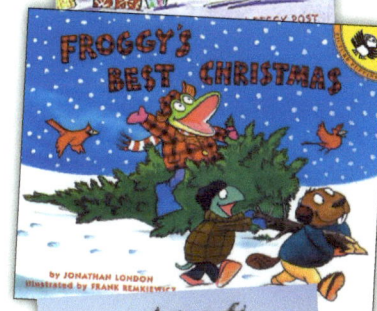

Froggy's Best Christmas

by Jonathan London and Frank Remkiewicz

Froggy usually sleeps through Christmas, but this year, his beaver friend wakes him up to join the fun. You can't beat a silly Froggy book.

Ages 3 +

The Christmas Wish

by Lori Evert and Per Breiehagen

Readers will be enchanted by the stunning photography in this Nordic holiday book. This is a precious story of a little girl who goes in search of Santa Claus.

Ages 3 +

ABOUT THE AUTHOR

Giselle Shardlow draws from her experiences as a teacher, traveler, mother, and yogi to write her yoga stories for kids. The purpose of her yoga books is to foster happy, healthy, and globally educated children. She lives in Boston with her husband and daughter.

ABOUT KIDS YOGA STORIES

We hope you enjoyed your Kids Yoga Stories experience. Visit *www.kidsyogastories.com* to:

RECEIVE UPDATES. For yoga tips, updates, giveaways, articles, kids yoga sequences, and activity ideas, sign up for our *free Kids Yoga Stories Newsletter*.

CONNECT WITH US. Please share with us about your yoga experiences. Send pictures of yourself practicing the poses. Describe your journey on our social media pages (Facebook, Pinterest, Twitter, Instagram, and Google+).

CHECK OUT FREE STUFF. Read our articles on books, yoga, parenting, and travel. Check out our free kids yoga resources and coloring pages.

READ OR WRITE A REVIEW. Read what others have to say about our yoga books and kids yoga lesson plans. Post your own review on Amazon or on our website. We would love to hear how you enjoyed these monthly yoga ideas.

Thank you for your support in spreading our message of integrating learning, movement, and fun.

Giselle

Kids Yoga Stories
www.kidsyogastories.com
www.facebook.com/kidsyogastories
www.pinterest.com/kidsyogastories
www.twitter.com/kidsyogastories
www.amazon.com/author/giselleshardlow
www.plus.google.com/+giselleshardlow
www.goodreads.com/giselleshardlow

YOGA STORIES BY GISELLE SHARDLOW

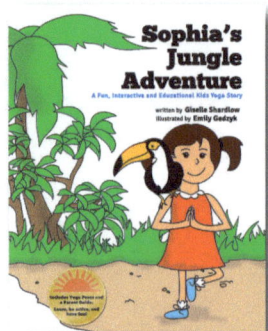

Sophia's Jungle Adventure

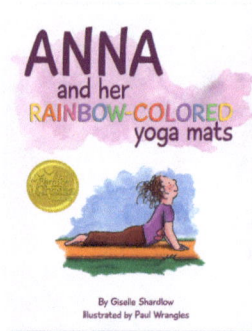

Anna and her
Rainbow-Colored
Yoga Mats

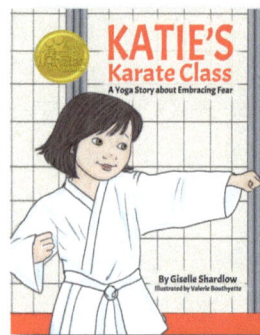

Katie's Karate Class

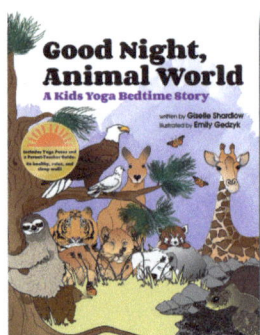

Good Night,
Animal World

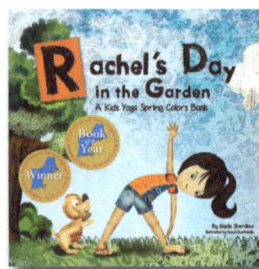

Rachel's Day
in the Garden

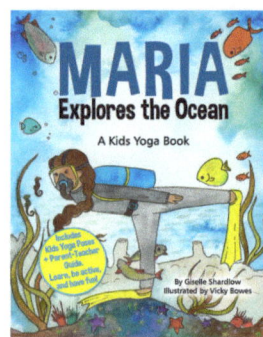

Maria Explores
the Ocean

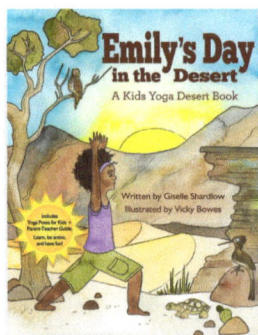

Emily's Day in the Desert

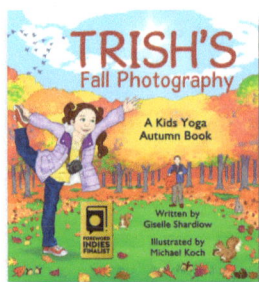

Trish's Fall Photography

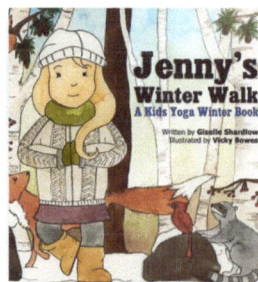

Jenny's Winter Walk

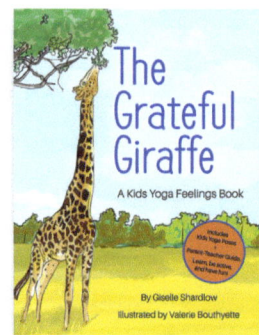

The Grateful Giraffe

OTHER KIDS YOGA RESOURCES

Yoga Poses for Kids Cards (Deck One)

Yoga Poses for Kids Cards (Deck Two)

Monthly Kids Yoga Themes eBook

Buy now at: **www.amazon.com/author/giselleshardlow**
or **http://www.kidsyogastories.com/store**

KIDS YOGA
STORIES

www.kidsyogastories.com

www.ingramcontent.com/pod-product-compliance
Lightning Source LLC
Chambersburg PA
CBHW042132070426
42450CB00002BA/87